A JOURNEY OF A THOUSAND MILES

Donovan G. Stokes

ISBN:1983558303
ISBN-13:9781983558306

It's All About Him Media & Publishing
P.O. Box 850
Paw Creek, NC 28130
www.aahmp.com
980-522-8096

Edited by Delisa Rodgers-Fields
Cover Design: Delisa Rodgers - Fields

To Gypsy & Jessi Shaw

OUR JOURNEY

I am writing this observation from my couch with the aroma of scented strawberries and cream candles flickering pictures across my naked walls. This sweet aroma sweetens my desire to share my heart by shading light exposing my shattered pieces. I have started my journey once again in hopes of bringing light towards drifting ships across the sea. I know all so well how it feels to paddle in the wrong direction; therefore, appreciating any glimpse of light shed through stained glass windows. As I sit in quiet stillness, I can sense a stirring taking place, not through keyboards and fingertips tapping to the rhythm of writers, but through a new beginning. This new beginning takes place where strong waves push the weight of heavy cargo ships loaded with life experiences towards that luminescent lighthouse. Skies that remained dark now clear, so rainbows can wrap themselves around bald eagles that scurry for food. With that in mind, I think of those who feel trapped in fleshly houses of melancholy, whose eyes swell with salty tears and cheeks that catches what they can before what's left fills cement cracks beneath tired feet worn from endless travels. So, would you, could you, break free as I did from the powerful grip of sadness? Or will you take up residence filling empty tombs that are not ready for you quite yet? Can you pull yourself up like tiny ants that are now able to lift what held tight to tree branches? Or will you continue to bury yourself alive without any unlocked doors to escape? I am guilty of cheerlessness and like seeds which claw their way towards the surface, I still have evidence of dirt between finger and nails as proof of my own struggle towards the light. While exposing my heart this way, I risk the chance of losing you but gaining you as well. How tragic will it be to lose you, to experience rejection for simply wanting to be free; yet how beautiful will it be if what is exposed strengthens you to row and not be eaten by whales fasting below the strong currents of living. Then my assignment is done when I witness your resurrection from the angry sea. I can finally breathe again through your nostrils. I can smile again when hearing not wailing but laughter spilling from your lips. I can continue writing if my words drain from my pulsating heart can rope you back towards safety. This is our journey.

ACKNOWLEDGMENTS

My journey could not be tolerated without those touchstones along my pathway who have proven to be a strong foundation, enabling me to stand when the storms of life blew my way. To Greg Pillar who has always been a sounding board when life required detours. To Monica Bitrick and Tami La Count for being great leaders by taking a chance to help me fly. To Steven Rosario who through constant encouragement, kept my heart listening to the rhythm of living in abundance. Awesome thanks to Robert W. Fuller for supporting, investing time, and offering sound advice towards investing in my own dreams as a writer and entrepreneur. To Nick and Tish for teaching me what it means to fight when the odds are stacked against me, I am so much better because of it. To my friend, Shane Michael Kinikin, for your patience and understanding, while I figured things out. To my stepmom, Toni Stokes, for the early morning manna needed to fuel my day. To my friend, Scott Jenkins, for motivating me to write even when he's not aware of it. To Mark and Laura for becoming my second pair of eyes. To the YMCA Learning Center family for strengthening our future generation through love and patience. And to my Grandmother, Irene Heyward, with whom this journey began.

You Are Beautiful Poetry On This Journey Of Mine

The Journey
Begins

Satisfied?

Why do we want the things we can't have and reject the things we have in hand? Once we are told the tree is forbidden to eat from intensifies the desire to taste the fruit. Stretching for ripened peaches hoping they would fall, makes a delicious peach cobbler for dinner but because those tree branches are unreachable, the frustration lies in changing the dessert menu to prunes while still having peaches on our minds. Can we successfully love one without longing after the other or will we always be this way?

What Truly Matters

The meaning of life is summed up in this small gesture of appreciation. Often when situations become confusing, I make my way to a nearby city park on the streets of Portland. This is where life unravels itself before my eyes, chasing away thick fog blinding the rays of the sun. Granted, it is these moments when clarity is needed to function properly and to see others, not as potential threats, but as welcoming invitations to a more enriching, uninhibited life.

Searching the majority of my life towards something or someone more fulfilling became an exhausting journey leading me where I first began. No amount of praise or adoration could ever fill those empty places lodged between what I know and what I am afraid to reveal. So, here I am where nature teaches me how to remain grounded yet growing deep beneath the landscape where tumbleweed dance in the wind. I am where I need to be to witness unshaped stones circumference wildflowers unashamed to bloom anyway, to witness this same concept walking the streets arm in arm engaged in conversations that truly matter. What draws me to this place is listening closely to my heart yell at my brain to escape in order to understand my place in the world, a place I constantly question while existing. Sitting quietly, I can hear Pandora from the bellies of birds that sing of summer long gone, calling for their sweethearts to return with great news of greener pastures where trees become stubborn, refusing to change because everything else did. I am to learn that when chaos chips away at my peace, to remain as I am, unbreakable like palm trees trapped in hurricanes. When depression attempts to molest my mind at midnight, stripping away my innocence, I am drawn downtown to see homelessness up close and personal. Then I am grateful for food and shelter. I complain less and worship more knowing that I am protected, not in sleeping on cold sidewalks, but smothered in love that warms my heart like feet in socks during winter time. While sitting, watching, and learning, I am compelled to look up instead of looking down on myself for not learning sooner. To see flying overhead an eagle cupping fresh food, dining sufficiently at the master's table and then to witness crawling at my feet little ants displaying their strength lifts me towards a clearer understanding of survival. Life is amazing and every breath that I take is love's way of keeping me here and grounded.

Snow

I love the snow if it means cuddling with a great book, wrapped in my favorite blanket like a butterfly hesitating to emerge. I love hot cocoa with marshmallows foaming at the top. I love the sound of a beating heart when quietness intensifies my passion for more. I love sticking my head out my front door feeling the snow landing and then melting across my freshly washed face. I love drawing hearts in the snow.

What Becomes Love?

The greatest love of all crawls through the darkness to feed the queen. It is the feel of another person's skin surrounded by soft music and scented candles. When water escapes the eyes of clouds, they dance across blades of grass before penetrating that fleshly wall called earth leading to the seed. When the moon cries for the sun and the wind caresses the faces of eagles, it then becomes love.

Overcoming Challenges

The challenges we experience are the same as the sun pulling back thick clouds preventing the land to grow. Grayish skies summon a gloom that affects the mood of existing. When this happens, thoughts and actions are clouded causing the heart to be indisposed for a moment. Struggles are a way of life for most things. Seeds, when experiencing pressure, crack open, bleeding beneath the soil. Everything seems fine above the ground until stripping back the layers reveal the violence below the leaves. Painful experiences are what defines character and strength.

When salmons become horny, they risk everything for a booty call. Hungry bears gather as eagles splatter, snatching the struggling salmon swimming against the stream. While some succumb to their sexual appetite, others survive making it to the other side. They learn what they thought was impossible to survive became another chapter in their birth of life. The example of these many challenges helps us to understand the importance of trying. When we fear trying, we cheat ourselves out of the opportunity to gain wisdom. If this happens, books like these never breathe on earth like wild weeds karate chopping concrete until it cracks, giving the sun the opportunity to kiss the seed that welcomes the flower. We are much better when overcoming our challenges.

Strength

The presence of yesterday lifts me up. I am as strong as you were the day before. I am standing because you lent your back for me to climb upon. I traced your spine with the essence of my feet to always remind myself to remain Strong. I am you, today!

(Photo Credit: gosbelherald.com)

The Benefits of Tears

If you're not able to cry, then how will your flowers ever grow? I know society would deem every man weak if tears escape their eyes. For real men don't cry and if you do, then you are a soft version of the truth. But, if tears ever moonwalk across your cheeks, then you will bountifully bloom where you are planted. And all those who experience your humility also flower in your garden.

Sex

The feel of love across my brown skin is rain showers across the green skin of new grass sprouting in the field. It's an indescribable feeling to have warm hands tiptoeing along the scalp of pores, tracing my spine bulging from my back. My need for touch whether on my juicy lips or behind my right ear is the thing that keeps me up at night. My heart gallops like wild horses free from human interference at the thought of your invitation to explore what makes me melt like hot fudge across vanilla ice cream. Now I know how the earth feels when rain penetrates the land.

I Love You

 If I can give the story any justice, I would try to explain how I feel when wind brushes against me. Words cannot express the tickling sensation I feel when I rest in dry leaves on Saturday afternoon or when it drizzles, and you drizzle on me. I can't put into words when the day drags on and I end my day in a grape-smelling bubble bath and when you hug me, my heart dances to the rhythm of your heartbeat. There aren't any descriptive narratives to explain how much I love the way you are.

The Tree That Stands Alone

I don't know about you, but when I find myself alone during difficult periods in my life when I really need to talk with someone concerning inward pain, my phone doesn't ring for days, my inbox remains empty after countless hello's and good mornings, and text messages come back unanswered. I shovel myself deep into the earth where roots cuddle at midnight. Seasons of change take place when all my green leaves are the color brown sleeping on the ground. But I remain standing, vulnerable for all to see and whisper and the awkwardness of all my branches, once hidden during the summer skies, no longer covers the sparrow's eyes. I am amazed, however how much I've grown and even though my season has changed, I will sprout again.

Beautiful Garden

It took me a long time to remove the weeds from my garden. Midnight tears moistened my field making it easy to remove what choked my daffodils. Now, I am free from what ails me, making my garden beautiful.

Love, Wind, and the Shoes They Wear

Where does the wind go when it first touches me? Does it walk or run, racing through the trees? If I had any say, I would think love was like this: invisible but very much real. Each step builds upon another in hopes of reaching towards the heart. My heart, your heart is the same creature hunted by treading feet upon stony surfaces...the wind goes, yet returns and touches again, again, and again in the same way love touches us all.

A World Full of Banana Peels

The world in which we live seems to unravel like delicious bananas in the hands of hungry school children. Without realizing it, banana peels settle beneath our feet making it slippery to maneuver. So, what are we to do when hatred like banana peels makes life difficult to walk in love? We walk together with caution, continuing to love as we go.

My Life

Schools of small fish speed swim through herds of great whites at the risk of getting eaten. Even though scary tornadoes twist and turn, rainbows in their confidence spit their colors anyway. Overcoming fear will determine successes. Our lives in three sentences...

Voices from the Ground

"Hello," from the ground I cried out often.

Entrapped by this shell in hopes that it softens,

To release what is hidden to experience what it must.

The sun and all its splendor, helped me rise from the dust.

The Land

Beauty is sketched across her canvas,

That silent breath became her language.

Forever will be and never forgotten,

Upon her face once scarred, bound, forgotten.

I Am the Seashell and the Seashell is Me

Deep within my soul resonates the sound of the deep where dolphins swim parallel against killer whales and seahorses clinging to drifting wood. As the sun sets and rises upon boisterous waves that soon die, vanishing between golden sand beneath my feet. I am the seashell and the seashell is me, so listen closely to the ocean singing from the deep.

Frozen Tears

Rain freezes before the earth drinks leaving the land unfulfilled again. While one stops giving, the other suffers and wails. Life beneath the cold winds wait with empty cups and promising dreams only to awake disappointed again. Tears fall only to freeze again like the day before because the sun refuses to penetrate gray skies that drape like heavy blankets over us. Will frozen tears become drinkable again? Will they ever slip through hands of innocence that play and splash in puddles watched by birds that wait their turn to bathe? And what about the earth that cries? Will the meadows protected under white hospital blankets ever thaw then sip? Who knows what will happen if the sun, like Moses, splits the ocean sky and warms all that breathes and sings? It is certain though that tomorrow will come and all that's hidden and forbidden will find their way to us, tanning again our faces while filling our bellies.

Inside a Rain Drop

To dance within a rain drop is to touch the hand of another separated by a transparent window. The only thing sensual about this touch is the remembrance of life in each other's arms. I have danced and cried within this clear morsel with visions of love unseparated. How can one breathe if hearts seem distant, no longer massaged by reality? Where have I gone if love doesn't exist in me?

Death

The past lounges in the mind and dances still. It steps to the beat of pounding drums in the hands, strong hands full of veins running to and fro from the heart. The present sun shines its way through dark corridors where furniture, like sin, rests in silence while in place. The future pushes her up from the ground, stretching her fingers where hot sand scorches beneath our feet. And all that remained alive in the mind dies by the touch of her hands.

Love Surfaces in Unusual Places

Love is found in unusual places. The priest and nun whose vows are interrupted by their secret passion for one another, hidden behind their priestly obligations to their church, are expressed between pews. Cracks erupting like miniature earthquakes freeing the seed to stretch where the air is soft upon her petals. Love, this emotion that can be both deadly and sweet like colorful snakes full of poisonous venom, is often drunk time and time again. The stream loves the rock that scratches their watery surface. The hurricane makes love to the ocean, one gives while the other receives, then strengthens before attacking the innocent bystander. Loves pulls tears or dries them depending on where we are.

Busy

Life is like living in New York City where people from all walks of life play bumper cars along busy sidewalks. No one really is talking except the music coming from their feet; everyone being in silent rhythm as they step one at a time. I see life this way where one life is its own individual, but everyone is doing it at the same time or not at all. I am constantly moving from one stage to the next, bumping into circumstances before reaching my destination. I notice the noise along my journey and wonder when will it stop screaming.

Friends

There are times in our life when the thought of expulsion lingers in the ax swung by others. Depression hits like a ton of bricks and getting out of bed is dreadful. When loneliness swells like broken ankles unattended, an unlikely friend spins along and saves the day. Where would we be without the Charlotte's in our lives?

(Photo Credit: childsplayaz.org)

Romanticism

I am guilty of being romantic because I see fields of wildflowers on train rides, birds washing the backs of the others in small pools of water trapped in cement cracks, and soft hands touching laps above the knee. The sun kisses the sky and the sky kisses the eagle and the eagle kissed the sunset and the sunset massages the achy muscles of towering mountains that lift me high to see.

I Found You

I thought I lost the sun when the clouds turned gray in my face. And through some miraculous afterthought, I realized that the sun was not lost but shaded, protecting my eyes from burning.

Touch Me

I awoke at 4 a.m., on Tuesday morning with this idea of touch on my mind. I walked outside, blending in with what was left of darkness being tracked by the moonlight and the feel of the wind grabbing parts of me forbidden to discuss.

I turned on the water sprinkler and listened how the earth passionately groaned as water spun in circle penetrating as it danced. It was then I understood the importance of embrace and how I longed to experience what green grass experienced wrapped in midnight blue.

For a moment, I disrobed completely and stepped in the way interrupting this romantic interlude and became like grass. I stretched my hands towards the darkened sky, gripping inquisitive stars while wetness folded between my toes. With my robe blanketing the earth, I was totally naked, drenched, and satisfied.

The Fight

A canoe full of people fighting the currents ending in a water fall can be both exciting and dangerous. Without the efforts of everyone involved, this could end disastrous for all who paddles and those who give in to exhaustion. But there are times in our lives when we are in the arena alone with the opposing side trying to knock us out of the fight.

(Photo Credit: nypost.com)

Winding Road

Trees overlap, touching above my head, blocking the sun as I trail along this path. With twists and turns in front of my feet worn by constant walking, I continued pondering what's on the other side of hills somewhat tampered by lost souls stumbling through the night.

I am those trees in knots preventing the sun from kissing my cheeks. I am the path like pretzels twisted at times, seasoned with salty tears. The only thing that satisfies really is a cold beer, but in my case, to dip my toes where the lighthouse knows how it feels. I am the hills with rough edges and slippery slopes, where close friends climb never making it to the top. For I am the tumbler whose candles flickers no more, waiting for that spiritual light.

Amazing Grace

The sea brushed against her washing away any sign of beachy sand clinging to her legs. She stood where we all stood once, gazing and hoping while standing on quick sand. The smell of seaweed and perfume shifted as the wind blew strands of brownish hairs from her eyes. It was towards the evening and the last song of seagulls vanished between thin clouds and golden sunset. Still, she gathered her thoughts and continued walking where land and sea collapsed within her footprints. Ripples created music against erected stone like monuments shielding that ocean from intruders except hers. She was welcomed. Her presence represented this need to explore from within all that happened and must happen to move forward. Life for her was like shipwrecked mini boat stationary where they rested. Beaten and abused, these somewhat shattered boats once dwelled upon the ocean filled with laughter and the possibilities of the unknown. Now, they slept upon the shores as distant memories, unfulfilled dreams where tiny sea creatures now take up residence. She did not take up shelter in broken down ships filling spaces along the shore but within her heart now shattered as a result of abuse. The sun slipped further as the moon grew brighter, illuminating her need to remain a little longer. Tears now flowed as the ocean flowed around her naked feet. In her desperation, she began to remove what little clothes she had on and made her way where ships once dwelled, and dolphins still kiss through the night. Into the cool water, she went, no longer warmed by the sun buried behind fallen stars. She dived deeper still trying to escape. The faster she swam away from the shores, the fainter the shores became. Her salty tears, now added to the ocean, creating a pathway towards liberation. Not only were her clothing like empty shells left along the scalp of the ocean, but her pain as well once covered beneath white satin and sunglasses.

Finally reaching the other side where the sand is much softer, much cooler, she washed ashore exhausted but relieved. Each awkward wave that pushed her where she ended, finally retreated back to its salty existence. She rested for a moment with her back against the cool sand with her feet still touching the water. It's as if parts of her didn't want to let go of the very current that shifted her along. At last on her feet, she began to travel again on the other side. With feet still wet, each grain of sand created a home between her toes making it difficult to maneuver but this voyage was necessary to finally free her from the past hoping to breathe again differently next time.

Upon removing her clothing and eyeglasses covering the sadness in her eyes, she continued to explore. Visible scars traced by the descending sunlight exposed her reasons for being there. What could be worse, the visible scars left behind by carelessness or the emotional bruises planted in place rooted deeply within her soul? Naked and vulnerable, she made no attempt to cover her shame. As the sun began to drift in the sea, a wisp of cool air ran its fingers through her hair. Even her salty tears created river beds within her gashes reminding her that the past was real and present. Still, she continued to move with such elegance leaving footprints in the sand.

"Where did I go wrong," she thought to herself as she wondered, listening to the sound of the wind whistling through the brush. Seagulls flew overhead snatching their last morsels before vanishing into the sunset. Dolphins sang and danced in the grayish blue sky before disappearing beneath the tides. Sitting now upon a rock, she noticed a torn piece of red sail drifting at her feet. She grabbed and wrapped herself with this faded material unraveling around its edges, blocking the wind that seemed fierce beneath the glittering moonlight against her skin. Resting for a moment, she began to think back on every episode of her life and just before she returned, a warm hand touched her shoulder from behind. It was an islander fishing off the banks that interrupted this flow of memories flooding her mind. He was golden in complexion with blue eyes seen only through thin layers of black hair waving like flags across his face. His gentle touch upon her shoulders separated the pain felt giving her relief for a moment. At one point, it seemed as if she wanted to reach out to him explaining her reasons for being there but instead, she lifted herself and ran without saying a word.

Exhausted, slowing her pace in time to notice small male crabs searching for mates, she too was in search for answers unrevealed back home. While the ocean continued to sing, brushing against her feet, she wrote her name in the sand. GRACE.

Grace was her name carved in wet sand. She found a broken branch drifted to land and began to tattoo her place in the world. A world that was full of hatred and abuse. This world unprotective of the underdog left her where she was, alone on that island.

Like brief moments of hard rain during long summer months, Grace always found herself running away from challenging situations. Escaping the reality of things into a world of fantasy was a coping skill developed from childhood. As a child, Grace would always volunteer to sit towards the back of classrooms in fear of being noticed. Growing up in a large family of five, and third, from the oldest, Grace never found the need to speak up for herself. As a matter of fact, before mustarding the strength to paint her language across the canvas of conversations, others would fill in her blanks leaving her once again without a voice. Many years later, her voice still remains hibernated behind layers of silence finally manifesting themselves on that deserted island desperately running from her past but presently leaving traces of her voice printed in the sand.

Exhausted from her escape, Grace ended up where we all end up when our resources become few and far between; where sun and moon speak briefly, take turns, before one vanishes leaving the other alone in that big dark sky above our heads. Grace, panting like thirsty deer startled by gunfire, set on a bending rock high above the ground yet low enough to see her reflection forming across shimmering waters guided by moonlight. While looking back at her reflection and carved out scars through her inability to fight back,

Grace realized that running away isn't the answer when fear continues to develop in utero. No amount of escape could ever escape that inner turmoil boiling within. Eventually, the seething pot simmering upon stoves violently explodes like volcanoes harming and destroying everything in its path. How can Grace, you and I, escape this concept? Where can we go without ourselves already being where we landed? Realizing what has happened and her inability to scream out loud her anguish, Grace leaped into the waters and swam back home.

Enjoying the Ride

On the subway of life, there are many seats filled with different lessons to learn. Some lessons expressed across the face, merely existing, show us how frustrated we become traveling in the same direction, perhaps falling to the same deception. Other lessons reveal to us how fortunate we are to have ridden at all.

My Life

Life doesn't make sense unless I see myself through an ant then I realize that I can carry more than my mind can comprehend. Life can seem challenging once pushed in the ocean now forced to swim with salmons. I know how strong I am as I wiggle, as they wiggle against the current to make it. Mistakes can feel dirty until I kick open the doors of my shell and dare whisper in the ear of the sun while hummingbirds rest upon my green shoulders drinking my sweet nectar. Life can seem gray until the wind blows the clouds away. Now things are clear, blue, and silky. For I am through all living things, abundant.

Inside of Me

What calms the sea dwells within me.

What causes the sun to shine, glow within me.

What beckons the tree to rise from the ashes, arise within me first.

What strengthens the ants to lift and carry, encourages me to lift myself from despair and carry love everywhere.

What fills ditches with fresh water, water springs my soul.

No More Regrets

If I can do this over, I would listen more, speaking less.

If I were five again, I would rest in my father's arms, smelling his masculinity.

If I was more courageous, it wouldn't matter what people thought about me.

If I were twenty-five again, I would have taken that job offer.

Spiritual Heart Surgery

The heart opens and sheds light and those of us left stranded in the dark, desperately search for our own doors we entered in so we can find our way towards love and light. This is the kind of surgery that will heal our contrite spirit.

I Am All of It

The extension of who I am is found overlooking the Atlantic Ocean in Charleston, South Carolina, with the smell of salt and clams hiding beneath moist sand where green grass tickles my ankles as I run uninhibited with sandals left behind. I am present. I am the ocean with secret wonders swimming through current tangled in floating seaweed. I am the bashful clam gripping magnificent pearls. I am the grass on the other side of parked cars. I am the salt that seasons the atmosphere. I am this ledge upon which I lean, and others leaned before me.

Fast Pace

There are times when life seems foggy and the only things seen are bright lights from very fast cars. What is seen soon disappears back in the dense reality of the hour glass. Like ducks that take off into the sky reflecting back in a lake, people are always in a hurry only to end up where they began. As hamsters spin on wheels, so do we spin collapsing going nowhere.

Greatness!!!

To dig up a seed before it has the chance to breathe is to betray the rose that could have bloomed. For mamma will never know the scent given from flowers performing their best resting on her tabletop. Why clip the wings of eagles destined to moon the sun? For greatness is found hidden between the petals where sugar brews, summoning honey bees to drink and the wings of birds with sharp beaks and eyes penetrating the Red Sea. So leave the seed, the eagle alone which thrives and flies within you and me.

Dad, My Lighthouse

The lighthouse watches as ships calmly grin in smooth sailing but something happens when white clouds turn gray and sunsets scurry in fear. The ship that sailed above killer whales suddenly disappears for a moment in boisterous waves stirred by His big spoon. All seemed lost, the captain and crew trying to make sense of it all, but just before coffins are ordered and grave plots are picked out, the lighthouse blazes and the ship sails safely home.

Life and Roller Coasters

At home today, I was thinking about my life. I call it a roller coaster with many twists and turns. Once I thought things leveled off, here comes another loop. Tears like morning dew layered my grass as friends came and went, some leaving me nauseous while others kept me laughing through unexpected turns. There were times I felt as if I plummeted without a secure seat belt to keep me grounded. All I could do was lift my hands, scream, and pray that I survive the next upside down… And I did…and YOU can too.

Taking Walks in the Dark

When the moon is hidden behind black scribble colored by God, I must find my way. Will it be easy? No. Will I cry, hitting my toe against cornered furniture resting in place? Yes. Maybe. Will others leave before the journey ends, when flashlights are buried beneath old papers and toolkits too difficult to find? Hard to say. When I walk alone in the darkness of my pain, when the moon slips and falls behind those darkened veils, finding my way isn't difficult if He remains my guiding light.

My Love Life

When I first laid eyes on this plant, I instantly fell in love with it. I come from a family of farmers, so I inherited my love for plants from their addiction to keeping their hands in the soil. This plant was given to friends of mine and it was beautiful at first. The leaves were big and green, and the vines seemed a mile long. This plant was fine at first, but something happened; the plant lost the attention of its owners. This plant, no longer green and full of vines, soon turned brown and brittle. This plant that once stood hanging over the window where the sun greeted us in the morning, hung in a cold garage waiting to be garbage. My first thought was to leave this plant in its misery, then I thought how I must look planted in my own soil. So, I reached out and grabbed this dying plant in hopes of restoring it

back to life. I clipped away all those lifeless leaves and watered and fed it. It wasn't long before strength was restored to those brittle vines producing beautiful leaves. Love nurtures back health to an individual left unattended. God wouldn't have it any other way.

Wisdom

To cling to that which is stronger is wisdom galloping through the land. I found this to be true as I rest my head upon the shoulders of experience.

(Photo Credit: quora.com)

The Ties That Bind

The day was bright and sunny and the clouds, which dangled overhead, stood still as to listen for their next commandment from God. Green trees danced romantically as a cool breeze made an unexpected visit. All the children in the area played in the streets disregarding the cars that passed by. It seemed as if they owned that street and each car was invading their territory. That street which held all those kids was an old remedy that healed one from the spirit of loneliness.

Many houses lined the edge of that street as to protect it from any type of invasion. Each home was so close to each other that it seemed like one house from a distance. Early in the morning, mothers holding their little ones on their hips could be found catching up with the latest gossip along the fences that separated their homes. This was a favorite pastime and a session was never missed. Fathers, on the other hand, rose early in the morning to catch the train to work. Hard hats and work boots flooded the streets while young and old men rushed off to make ends meet. "Ends," one would grumble, "never meet," but the thought of having a job was considered a blessing in disguise. Yes, times were hard for American families and one would expect it to get worse before becoming better.

On one side of those narrow roads, stood a tavern and every day before those tired men returned home from work, they would stop there to talk about their ill treatment on their jobs. This gathering was a social place of relief because one man's issue became every man's issue. Upon returning home, many of those men found their homes sending smoke signals into the air letting one know that supper was being prepared. Fathers would walk into their homes finding their children sitting, doing homework while mother stood in a hot kitchen with the smell of fried chicken popping in hot grease. Mothers, throughout the community, could be heard sending up a wailing as hot grease popped the surfaces of their skin. Nevertheless, everyone was anticipating a delicious meal for it was at the dinner, everyone could find out the latest scope in the neighborhood.

As mothers, fathers, sons, and daughters gathered around the dinner table, one would have the honors of saying the dinner prayer before eating and if not said correctly, mother would reach over and pinch the most honorable grace sayer. Once seated at the dinner table, a moment of silence took the stage and an applause or two could be heard in the mind of each spectator. No one responding yet, but the munching sounds made harmony and echoed throughout the room. Mother, every now and then, could be found gazing to see if her cooking was a success. The silence was an indication that all was well and the words, "Can I have seconds?" were soon to come.

Before dinner was over, one brave soul would break the moment of silence. Usually, it would be one of the children with some awkward story concerning events that took place at school. But this time, it was dad. Dad had a deep voice that carried through the room like lightning. Whenever dad spoke, one was sure to listen because he was the man of the house and whatever dad said was of importance. Dad's voice was like God speaking to Moses on Mt. Sinai. Each word seemed to penetrate the very depths of one's soul. "How was your day?" he would ask and everyone like a harmonious ensemble would answer at the same time in one key "Fine................"

Next, mom would go into what was going on in the neighborhood. She would start off by asking, "Did you know that, Mrs. 'So and So' did this," and "Mr. 'So and So' did that?" Dad would then respond with great expectations and listen attentively as she unraveled the mysteries of the neighborhood. Many yawns came forward as an indication that sleep was necessary to begin a new day. Before going to bed, all the children would brush their teeth while mom put away the dinner dishes. Dad would be out back either smoking a cigarette or cleaning off his work boots for the next dreaded day ahead. Going from day to day was always a day of mysteries. The expectancy of each moment was tattooed across the heart of individuals as the clock quickly ticked through the silence of the night.

The sweet aroma of prayer began to fill the room as each individual bowed before God, thanking Him for what He had done and what He was going to do. God was the center of that community and their closeness was due to their constant involvement with the Almighty. Broken hearts, sickness, death, and abandonment pulled tears from the foundation of their soul with a strong belief in prayer for something greater. And like this family, we all can face another day with this same assurance.

Honesty and Openness

Love feeds on honesty and openness like an infant child who feeds on simple formulas to protect its delicate digestive system. Honesty and openness act as vitamins that revitalize the human body. With each swallow of these two substances, the spirit becomes dependent on this miracle drug. Without honesty and openness, the spirit feels the effects by becoming sluggish, not fully capable of trusting. The willpower to endure an everyday task brings the mind back to where it needs to be. However, if openness and honesty remain stubborn, love finds it difficult to perform fully, therefore, anticipating an unkind behavior.

Almost Fall

As summer kisses the feet of Fall, golden chocolate chips melt in my mouth. I am saddened to see come to an end green leaves fading into the color red. Although Fall is my favorite season, I will miss running across the warmth of sand between my toes towards that liquid glass holding hostage that ball of fire from the sky. Green grass will finally sleep beneath their blankets made from dead leaves dancing in the wind. And I get to remain, I hope, to see.

Trauma Free

Give and it shall be given, seek and ye shall find, knock and the doors shall be open unto you. The doors of opportunities shall be open unto the one who gives. Not being afraid to give brings about change. When one gives, it is a yielding of one's control of hurt, pain, rejection, and shame. These traumas are hidden on the inside and do not want to be disturbed. But, when those doors are opened, these traumas combine forces and do their very best to stop one from giving of themselves. It is a shame what past hurt can do to an individual who only wants to be free. When one grabs the knob of expectancy and opens the door of opportunity, victory takes over. However, in order for victory to happen, one must be tired of bondage. Because of this, revolution against bondage celebrates healing in our midst.

Storms

Fight against the forty day and forty-night storm that came to trouble Noah and his family. Like the children of Israel who wandered forty years in the wilderness or even like Jesus who was tempted by the opposition, we must fight like a madman who finds himself trapped in a corner and the only way of getting out is through swinging. Fight for your life, dignity, and normality. Don't throw in the towel when it seems that the odds are against you. Don't give up on those things that will hurt and haunt you farther down the road where it's almost impossible to see treacherous roads where winding curves get steeper and steeper. Be careful though, for this drive is driven by faith and like Noah, we are protected through the storm.

UNO!!!!

Life can seem like UNO cards. Just when one thinks he or she would win the game by bellowing, "UNO," being one card away, someone interrupts this potential win with an unexpected Draw Four in hand. When this happens, Reverse your unhappiness, Draw Two breaths, Skip all complaints by loving on the Wild side...this is one sure way to win the game.

Mamma — Dedicated to Irene Hayward

The news of grandma's death started in a child's dream months before the actual event. While the moon guarded the sky at night and morning glories locked their doors, I was fourteen when this happened and unprepared to say goodbye. This vision was not expected; this dream I didn't understand woke me in the silence of night. Eyes full of tears were wiped away as I slowly interpreted this dreadful dream. Halloween costumes filled the stores with fragments of Thanksgiving napkins along with matching table clothes accented with Christmas ornaments filled each shelf, but this dream closed my eyes, seeing nothing but empty shelves missing her already. Trick-O-Treat and the smell of turkey and dressing slowly faded into the sounds of Christmas Carols when it happened. My dream, like the wind, blew what was left of history from my family tree. I cried at the thought of her not being here especially since my birthday was eleven days away.

My Grandmother, known as "Mamma", was considered my best friend. It hurt me deeply not to be in her presence, but I suffered through until my grief, like wounds, scabbed then healed. Whenever you saw Mamma, you saw me whether hanging around in the kitchen, feeding her cats, clipping her toenails, or combing her salt and pepper hair. I was there because I needed her protection. Like a queen bee, Mamma was center of her colony and I delighted to be there when she delegated her authority. Mamma was very strict but delicate. Beneath her words and each mission heralded from her voice was carried out without questions. Yes, there were times when I thought Mamma was mean and insensitive, but something about her made me love her even more.

I remember when mamma and I would sit around the kitchen table. Well, I sat, but Mamma simply leaned over the table with her elbows pressed so hard against the table's hard surface that it left imprints on her elbow making them calloused. We gathered and talked, smoking cigarettes, as she opened up about her life as a child living in the country. We laughed and laughed, reminiscing about those good old days. Thinking back on those days in Grandma's kitchen brings laughter to my saddened expression even now. Also, I remember sitting in church and nudging Mamma to stay awake while the pastor preached the Sunday morning message. I enjoyed those times in church, watching the church mothers dressed in white, shout, and praise God for all He's done in their lives. My Mamma was among those saints who danced like David before God while at the age of seven, I found myself tapping my feet and nodding my head from side to side like I was watching a tennis match at Wimbledon. I also remember those spankings, or should I say beatings I received when I stole money from her purse, pocketing coins to buy pickled pig feet and five cent butter cookies from the nearest corner store. Regardless of how severe her spankings were, I clung to Mamma and her teachings of life lessons even until that day when my rendezvous with death invaded my territory.

Like a hail storm that beats against a house so did that dream I had. Even though I went throughout the day tending to my chores, that dream remained stubborn like dried food stuck to frying pans. Nothing I said or did could shake green leaves from a vibrant tree. One day I received a phone call from Mamma and the conversation started out the same as it always did. "How are you?" Mamma would always say with her deep voice. "Fine," I said, still thinking about the inevitable. Even now remembering that phone call which was the last time I heard her voice, I wondered if she somehow received that same message and in some mysterious way was letting me know that our time was coming to an end.

The day Mamma died, we had just put up our Christmas Tree. Trying to adjust an old artificial Christmas Tree was not agreeing with my perfectionist personality. The door swung open and there was Mamma. We all greeted her as she entered the house before she sat down near our television set. Ten minutes after her arrival, Mamma closed her eyes like a beautiful sunset during Indian summer. This was her way of quietly prying open the doors of life and slipping peacefully into eternity. The news of her departure was announced hours later on December 3, 1984.

The announcement did not come as a shock to me. I knew months ago that this event would take place. Mamma is with the Lord now and even though she is not here, her memory lives on in the lives of her colony. Years later, that dreadful dream remains rested in my mind. Mamma's life and death has taught me something professors could never teach, and that is, as challenging things may be at times, life is very precious. No one really knows how long we have on earth with family and friends. So, we must live our lives as if it were our last and the dreams we have concerning the ones we love won't leave a string of regrets behind. Having strong connections always soothes those dreaded dreams given through the night.

Cross

Colorful paint stains my clear windows. Each color glazed across my once clear transparency has baffled me through the years. One stroke at a time signified moments of lonely fear and unstoppable tears. But as I gathered my stained-glass windows and glued them together by insurmountable strength buried within, I realized my concealed strength summoned this bright light revealing my hidden cross.

The Finish Line

God peaked over the clouds just in time to catch a man tying his shoes. He blew His breath that sent the man galloping along the way like wild horses do when startled. Each stride the man took represents hurdles in his life. Sweat drenched his face as an indication of some form of struggle resulting in his desire to win. His knees ached as he stretched with stride. He wiped the sweat from his brow so he could see his opponents. He glided through God's sweet breath with confidence just like eagles that flap their wings in spite of angry clouds spitting rain in their faces. Some, the man thinks to himself while running, cheer him on while others simply mock him. His cheerleaders celebrate him for not being consumed by the agony of bitterness while others ridicule him for refusing to give up. The trap that was set before him didn't work because he knew all the right steps to make. When God exhaled, the runner simply took advantage of the opportunity and hurdled over every verbal abuse. Sure, the man was hurt as he ran this race, but God kept His eyes on him. Every stride the man took was not always perfect; there were times when aches and pain beckoned the man to stop. He could hear his own breath out-sing his heart as his tired feet violated the streets. Others running alongside him whose sweat flew in his mouth tasted salty as they leaned over and smiled at him when the finish line became visible with their naked eyes. Yet God continued to peek between the clouds blowing kisses helping that exhausted man win the race.

An Orange in a World Full of Apples

What's wrong with being different? Are you afraid others would laugh at you for having darker skin or longer legs or red hair or no legs?

How do you think broken trees feel, cut down at the trunk between two oak trees who stand tall, tickling heaven's armpits with their long fingernails? They don't care! For their roots trail the underworld, drinking quietly sugar's rays filling their bellies. They sing songs of victory while new life springs from their wombs. Not before long, what was announced as broken and different, produces Vitamin C, healing the lives of many.

Dad

Strong, black, and powerful is what I remembered. An occasional hug is rehearsed in my mind. A young boy needs his dad as he tiptoes through life's mysteries. Bullies are intimidated when dad's around. Bedtime stories come to life when dad reads out loud. The scent of cologne fused by the smell of sweaty musk indicates that daddy's home and all is well now. Hard work carved between the lines in his hands feel good upon my head for a job well done. Muscles bulge through his shirt signifying outer strength with his heart beating strong, motivating us all to be strong.

Yes, I needed my father. I felt alone and needed that empty feeling to be filled with his reassurance. I always felt alone. I walked alone, I ate alone, and I cried alone but mended the way he wanted me to.

I always envied children and their dads and even though I am older and a lot more mature, I sometimes find myself longing for his embrace. How children and their dads communicated, laughed, and played embedded my secret place, a place where no one dares to enter. Being in the same room with my father was the cure needed to rescue me from an invisible foe.

Being taught to share or tie a tie was done by my own need to fantasy his presence. Smiles broke through my flesh at an occasional past memory exploding in my mind. Those distant memories rescued me from self-destruction. My father was and is a man who felt he was and is better than the average and when he could, tried to install those principles within his offspring. Looking back at those years, I realize that I missed out on a lot, and time, that cruel ticking of the clock, does not allow any of us to go back and scoop the sand that slips through the hourglass. I do however have this time to reminisce and to attempt to gain as much now as I could have received back then.

Life is too short and the words, "I love you," minimize the hurt that tries to strangle any form of reconciliation. For when one vanishes like puffs of smoke from a lit cigarette, he or she cannot give nor receive the forgiveness needed to thrive again. For I refuse to allow those unspoken words to remain forever trapped behind decaying flesh tucked away beneath the soil. I have my dad now and the angels are rejoicing.

Adapting to Change

How do I explain how I feel when many changes are taking place at the same time? The feeling that overwhelms, caps my emotions as I sit here writing another episode of my life. Family and friends seem distant when going through the valley. Smiles and tears all mixed together make their guest appearance all at once. Loneliness whispers sweet nothings in my ear as I stand mesmerized by its allusive words. The solitude of peace is interrupted by the chaos of my changes.

Change is a good thing. Winter's bitterness slowly fades into the background as springtime life awakens. A man falling in love and marrying the person of his dreams thinks of his future while waltzing down the alley. Children quickly race to the waterhole down below trying to beat the summer heat, laughing at the thought of summer vacation away from school. A husband and wife or partner looking over their newborn child with the thought of lunch boxes and college tuition are excited yet nervous about their change. Why then am I not excited about mine?

Dealing with the unknown is scary. Going to an empty apartment day after day, I often grieve for the voice and breath of another. Hearing another's voice soothes that savage beast trying to discourage me. My environment, called that silent person, teases and taunts me until tears are extracted from my eyes. But love is always there blowing my sails, comforting and leading me to a place that is higher than I. This place (my soul) is where silence is replaced with laughter and the echoes of thriving hearts.

Skating Across the Sky

While in the air sitting between two passengers and the taste of pretzels and ginger ale colliding in my mouth, I had time to think. I thought about life on the other side of clouds that imprinted as we traveled. Below, where storms invade the sky, is no comparison to the other side. If only I can ascend like airplanes do when focused on their destination so I can experience how clear the skies in my life can be. With engine parts all working together reassuring our safety, my safety is a prime example of all those in my life who worked together pushing me past my stormy past towards blue clearer calm. I am thankful the more of watching others interact with those whose hearts relish the other's presence. Life is full of love given and received and written across these pages. And soaring beyond where I was is only the beginning, and witnessing where I am heading is worth the adventure.

Step by Step

When I have the opportunity, I will dance more often to the beat of living. Each step towards my destination is a celebration of breathing. Trees understand this by the waving of their hands while the wind whispers in their ear. Will flowers finally get on their feet two-stepping at every beat? Never again will I sit in silence missing my song.

Each Generation Deserves to Breathe

Buried beneath the depths of land are seeds unharmed by fire. Those who stand and touch the sky must burn giving in to sorrow. But when they do shout and cry, this gives the unborn their try.

Breaking is Necessary

When dolphins break the hymen of blue seas, bleeding reveals tampering. I am often reminded of innocent things becoming violated in the purity of beginnings. When green meadows become bombarded by soda cans and empty potato chip bags, this disfigures the beauty of the land. As a result, I understand that my mind can no longer go back where things seem simple and normal. What breaks, destroys the calmness that sunsets bring before bright stars bombard heaven. The good news is that whatever breaks, returns to some aspect of normal.

Forever Surfacing

The conditions of our lives rest between the cracks in our hearts; for loving or hating stands upon our abilities to feel the currents that flow with our joy or sadness. What has surfaced are the results of what lingered between what gives way. If I am bombarded with negative emotions, an explosion is just a matter of time and all those left holding awkward pieces of my puzzle barely escape alive. This then summons my need to explore meaningful poetry by finding ways to become a beautiful poem.

Breathe

The more I continue to breathe, the more I understand how short life is. I have made it a point to always count the stars at night and realize that the darkest of days produce the brightest of stars, to always look up during the day hoping to see birds flying then disappearing where the sun kisses the Adam's Apple of towering mountains mesmerized by the shimmering sea which confounds me. And when I feel alone or embarrassed for feeling anything at all, I inhale and exhale to breathe again.

Letting Go What Refuses to Break

Winter breeze shake what's left of brown leaves refusing to let go. He was like that. Saturday after Saturday, he found himself at that local café on the corner where little old ladies found it difficult to cross those busy streets. Life was very challenging as he tried to make sense of it all and the circumstances surrounding his need to sit and stare. Before that chair occupied his presence and the sadness of his expression tattooed those windows, life was beautiful before the accident.

In the beginning, life was tolerable. With kids screaming between food fights and the smell of shaving cream and bacon colliding in the atmosphere, life became what it was. Normal. Children grabbing backpacks, his wife standing at the door holding lunch boxes before a yellow bus took them away, and he was always the last one to leave. With a kiss on her lips, that warm kiss he remembered as he drove down the street constantly being interrupted by stop lights and morning traffic jams always seem to help him maneuver through the chaotic day ahead. Who would have ever known that the sound of children, his children, and the feel of Cheerios crushing beneath his freshly polished, black alligator shoes would vanish like that warm kiss he often remembered when nights became restless and the only way to sleep now was through masturbation.

I know. I know, too much information, right, until it hits your home and all that's forbidden finally becomes reality staring you in the face. He thought the same way, at least from what he was taught in Sunday School. Life was to be a pathway, not to hell but heaven and in reality, hell becomes that open gate leading to a richer more meaningful life only in time, though.

At first, it's painful, like a strong wind gnawing away at leaves whose season has ended. The wind knows it except the leaf that struggles to remain attached but is no longer being fed. It hurts to finally realize that what was held dear no longer supports your reasons for living. His life changed when the phone rang.

After receiving that call, the phone dropped from his right hand across the floor where he landed. Tears flooded his meadows and up popped choking weeds smothering what took time to sprout from cow manure. They were all gone. Just like that, his life transformed and learning to breathe differently became his main objective. "How can things change so fast?" he thought to himself, trying to understand this curveball thrown in the middle of the game. One minute his life was full of laughter and questions such as, "Whose turn was it to take out the garbage?" to the silence of once occupied tenants whose face was his face looking in the mirror.

"How can I stand now upon stable foundations while they slept prematurely in their graves?" he muttered to himself. "Where has the wind carried me but upon dead leaves towards the end of fall? Can I walk alone now with broken fences outlining my journey?" Debris has shifted his way, distorting his view of things. Garbage stacked upon garbage continued to stink his existence to live without them.

One beautiful day and a couple of drinks, bourbon according to the reports, shattered all hopes and dreams of brighter days ahead. The gentleman responsible had just ended a thirty-year marriage and found comfort at a local bar. Drink after drink, he jumped into his car, spun his wheels, and destroyed the lives of those hoping to reach adulthood. Their mother, this poor man's wife behind the wheels, died instantly, probably all for the best so she didn't have to witness her kids bleeding beneath white sheets.

After reading those horrible reports from that local café, he left his papers across the table and out the door he went. "I can't go home," he whispered between the sounds of distant conversations and sirens flooding the streets. He jumps into his car joining countless others fighting heavy traffic making his way to the other side of town where it was quiet and less distracting. There, the man could reflect on which direction to go without the support he once had.

It's difficult to move forward without a strong current to lift the heavy weight we bear. Finding the courage to breathe anyway as the wind ceases for a moment then changes directions carrying within its bosom garbage instead, is the thing we all dread and accept. The man, like we all, must continue living in a world whose invisible hand controls the light switch. Darkness drapes our small living spaces distorting our view of things but thereafter, the light comes on and we find our exit. The misfortunes of this man represent all of us dealing with a loss of some kind, but we can find comfort in knowing that the upside down of losses are the insurmountable possibilities of loving again only if we dare to.

Old and New

Just because leaves fall from your tree, doesn't mean your tree is dead. Your tree, like snakes between two rocks, must rid themselves of the old, making room for the new. So free yourself from the tight opinions of others even if it leaves you naked.

Once Living in Silence

Why live in silence when everything speaks? The clouds speak when it cries on Monday mornings. The earth speaks by giving back colors that drape her nakedness. The way tree branches break, speaks volumes of pain causing owls to have no stages to sing their melody. Even the heart tells stories during the night while the moon shines brightly as darkness escapes through half-open windows. Cell phones ring breaking the silence of quiet text messages and we respond to them all.

The Death of Seasons

When it dies, bury it. Dig a hole, place it in the ground, and cover it. A relationship, for example, at first gave you orange juice, full of essential vitamins like love, peace, and joy but it now serves you lemons riddled with bittersweet memories. Sure, you may stand alone like an open barn in the woods surrounded by possible creatures that wander in. Tears may flood ditches, which turn into lakes, which turn into oceans. That which glimmers in the moonlight turns green around your neck. Know when to let go. Know when the season's change and leaves aren't strong enough to cling to their branches. Understand the shift like an underwater Titanic making U-turns. When there isn't any heartbeat, pull the plug and sing a song.

Double Life

To live two lives is to be split down the middle, sharing the same heart. How can one heart hold the lives of two different people? Can the heart keep rhythm by constantly performing before a different audience? To be two different people at once is for a rose to bloom, then eat house flies for lunch like a Venus Fly Trap. I say as we deal with our own double standards, let's fuse into one and hug.

The Heart is a Puzzle

It's ludacris to make chicken salad without chicken as it is insane to love but hate your lover. The missing ingredient always spoils the potential meal for others to enjoy. I know all so well what life was like operating with a numb heart. Smiling but hurting. Content yet restless. Counseling but needing counseling. Puzzle almost completed except for one missing piece but then understanding that life is always full of unexpected turns in the road and if I am to experience completion, I must truly be honest by investigating that missing piece.

When My Leaf Fell

When a leaf falls, I am reminded of the day I fell. It was a cold winter's night when Christmas tree lights blazed through windows. I was green like a leaf blowin' in the breeze now brown fallen to the ground. All things come to an end as I think about it now. What once blocked the heating sun from scorching the land, now dangles, fading quickly. Holding on to life, the leaf grips harder to its mother that provided nutrients and security. The leaf remembered how it felt feeling the wind along its belly which now cradles it to the ground. There it rested at her feet watching new life take its place. The changing of seasons hurt at times but necessary in learning the lesson. I definitely understand now that things must change and letting go is part of the process. As this leaf broke free from strong winds determined to help it fly as birds fly, when my turn came, nothing held the wind from snapping my cords so that I could join others like myself. I am now settled in my spot which beckoned me from the beginning. For like that leaf, I am where I need to be, free from experiencing that again. And when strong winds blow, releasing your leaf to join our pile, together we will share our stories.

Images Through My Own Eyes

I have spent my life looking through other people's windows. Don't get me wrong, I am not a Peeping Tom but windows, meaning their eyes looking back at me and I at them...and what did I see? Perhaps a valley of dry bones or a superhero in midair. Regardless of the image from what others can see, I am uniquely who I am looking back at me through my own eyes happy as can be.

Without Love

If it never rained, tomato plants would die, and the meadows would cease to carry wildlife hidden among the grassland. I believe we would die if love no longer carried our need for intimacy. We would be like Forrest Gump trying to outrun his memory of making love to Jenny the night before. The wind would shift us from one hurricane to the next never experiencing the calm within the eye of the storm. Life, in itself, remains difficult, choosing from a box of chocolates hoping to get the one filled with walnuts and caramel but instead, receiving the one filled with orange sugar covered in chocolate. Without rain, without love, we would never grow but expire like rose bushes whose petals are too weak to hold the fragile legs of bumblebees. Quickly, we would fall apart, covering our flower beds with layers of crumbled leaves once hugging their branches. As humans, we must have this emotion, this strong emotion if we are to continue in peace and not kill each other.

Depression

Depression smears her grayish paint across a clear canvas. It will not allow one to see the yellow sun smiling back at us wrapped in her favorite rainbow blanket. Covers become heavier trying to free oneself from his wrath. I know how this feels as I push away those blankets hoping to make a dash for it. Instead, I find myself held hostage by this melancholy. This microscopic unhappiness creates an enormous amount of pain. Even sweet music sounds bitter in my ears when I am crestfallen. I am in need of relief to feel jubilant again.

A Hungry Sea and the Pain We Bear

On the seashore of new beginnings rests the subtle footprints left behind by individuals whose life, like waves, sweeps then returns to lick the rest. The past loves to hunt and capture its victims unaware of its presence. It pulls the trigger, piercing the heart until it no longer receives a pulse. No wonder walking helps clear the mind filled with pain that still lingers long after it happens. The sea teaches lessons about what happens when watery fingers scrape away those gentle feet held by heavy hearts. The wet sand represents our past and the footprints represent those stubborn stains that try to leave their tattoo on our beaches. That's when a strong wind heralds from a split in the clouds causing the waves of forgiveness to digest our past back into the sea.

Experiencing Transitions

Don't hate me because I'm gold, no longer green. For I have a gift to transition from one color to the next. Although I'm tall and soon to be naked, never try to figure me out. My color will leap from a frog's back one moment and shine like a gold ring around your finger the next moment.... why? Because I am free to be me.

Rescued

If we stand still lost in the woods, all we have to do is stay put and love will find us. But if we continue to wander in unfamiliar territory, it becomes difficult to locate our whereabouts. Too often, we venture out where shrubs grow wildly in our way. It's not their fault; they follow direction from beyond the clouds, it's ours. Becoming lost in hatred and animosity pushes us deeper into the woods. The light appears dimmer trying to shine where trees spread their wings. The sound of undomesticated animals can be heard licking their lips in hopes of finding a meal. The more we wonder, the more we risk the chance of standing in harm's way. But if we dig our heels into the soil of our spirit and stand our ground refusing to move forward with revenge, love locates, shines her light, and rescues us in time.

Cancer

Hate is cancer in its last stages. It eats away at the very organs designed to keep us functioning. One moment we are upright until disappointment alters how we think and feel, by then it's too late. Or is it? To love through hate is the chemotherapy hooked to our veins to keep us alive. Some shed their hair which covered the beauty of their eyes while others continued to hide behind the strains of their crown. Love slips through our veins causing us to lose what burdens us. Each layer hits the ground freeing us from combing this strong emotion responsible for doing further damage. Yet there are others determined to remain as they are full of animosity swiftly dying.

Winter Seeds

 I am the seed that waits beneath the harsh of winter. I remain huddled in my casing trying to keep warm like male penguins cuddling while waiting for the birth of their children. Never worry because my time will come when what awaits finally appears and laughs. My arms will stretch hugging the sun; my legs will grow once occupied by snow. My pores will give birth to green leaves supporting ladybug eggs. Just wait and see.

Nature's Gentle Sermons

The place I find the best of me is in nature. Taking a walk in the great outdoors clears my mind of the chaos left behind that haunts me throughout the night. Nature is where God displays His beauty and I am an active participant in all He has to preach. I learn when I approach a tree with broken limbs that as long as I remain rooted and grounded, it doesn't matter how my branches sway. As I continue to travel, summoned by a beautiful lake, I take the time to view my own magnificence across her liquid pores. And when the threat of negative words (a type of terrorism) try and destroy my self-esteem, I quickly return to the very place where God took His picture of me. Facing a stone chipped away from nearby mountains, I see my own heart in surgery being drilled, chipping away at all those hardships that once left me calloused. The sound of rushing water bashing against rocks soothes those rough edges and when faced with challenges, I must become like water bashing and soothing against and upon those jagged edges of others.

Small animals that have decayed along the way became nature's way, through death and fertilization, of producing more colorful, stronger wildflowers. This concept has quickly brought to mind those rotting situations in my own life that died in order to enrich my soil, producing sweet aromas of second chances.

Nature is my church and when I sit quietly in His pews upon my bench, His message whispers through my ear and I continue to bloom.

The Pain of Building Fences

The more we build walls around our hearts avoiding emotional pain from others, we make it difficult for love to enter in. How can we experience the gift of love when we are constantly digging barriers like grave diggers? A dagger pierced through the heart creates such agony that the only way to survive is to bury deep within the earth where the sun struggles to kiss the seed. Covering ourselves is easy but not easy enough for love to scrape away dead layers of skin that causes irritation. The more we hammer and nail pieces of wood together without paying attention to the lesson needing to be learned, our once thriving heart fails to thrive and becomes crippled. If that happens, we become paralyzed, unable to feel the gentle touch of joy trying to recapture the strength that pulsates between the pores of our existence to be happy. In fact, I understand how unhappiness blocks the light because when suffering pain, I retrieve in the night rejecting the light. Even though I felt safer that way, I missed countless opportunities of wholesome relationships able to lift me up. And when I am lifted, the closer I am to that which makes me stronger.

Looking back on those turbulent years motivated me to build fences all around me, consequently causing many years of loneliness. If we are to ever experience the joy of loving, we must begin by tearing down all efforts of protecting our hearts from the lessons that make us wiser.

The Pearl in Me

The oyster must tolerate the sand and the sand must sleep 'till morning and when the alarm clock rings, the pearl inside the sand awakens. I find this to be true in my life as I continue to muster through every phase with gratitude. Feeling worthless or useless or both has tagged along for the ride. When I find myself in total solitude, clearing my mind from the toxic pollution of negativity, I must remember the pearl. How can a small grain of sand become something of significance? How does destiny choose one golden grain of sand from among trillions bathing along the scalps of oceans? Maybe that's the lesson, to find myself incarcerated by what ails me in order to see who I truly am.

When looking in the mirror, I am horrified by what I see. Doubt and disappointment accompanied by this unending feeling of failure have blurred my vision, so remembering the process is very vital to my well-being.

The sand finds no escape once enclosed. Perhaps through yawning, the oyster swallows the sand and becomes irritated by its invasion. Through my journeys, I had become very irritated by things disrupting my comfortable lifestyle. Like rubbing against sandpaper, frustration loomed over me creating lonely days and sleepless nights. Great advice from meaningful people in my life slipped through my ears like water in a cup turned upside down. But then I realized that all things are lessons that God would have us learn and like the sand that frustrates the oyster, the oyster frustrates the sand by refusing to let go. Now I see myself as the oyster that clings to things unnecessary, so I thought. I also see myself as the sand trapped for not paying attention but when I remained still and chased away the noise that beckons confusion in my life, I emerged as the pearl emerges from what seemed impossible.

Where I Belong

As I bake in the sun across the golden sand of Florida's coast and feel that miniature wave between my toes, I listen very carefully to beautiful mermaids singing in the wind. It is these moments when getting away finds me where I am. When the mood of the day shimmers in the sun as it is peeking through the clouds, while my legs and arms remain stretched, and while lying on my back feeling wet sand trace my spine, I am relieved to know that when I am thrust into chaos, I can close my eyes and return where I belong.

Sticks and Stones

How strong are my bones which hang my chocolate jacket? Every bone connected to the other doesn't argue concerning their differences in appearance but joyfully work together protecting my vital organs. My heart, for example, remains unharmed, pulsating behind my rib cage hidden behind my nipples. And stones, adjacent to the others, kiss the sky and become home where eagles die. But when sticks and stones crush my bones, they trigger the agony of pain 'till healing comes, but negative words not only crush but consequently linger.

What Happens When You Bake a Caterpillar?

When the heat of living is turned up by human hands and empty bellies, the batter rises, swelling in the pan. It doesn't take much to heat a small room. Finding yourself cramped because your turn has come to change is something we all experience. A lover who disappears with your gifts in her hands is enough to make any man cry. Temperature rises motivating the opportunity to beat the shit out of those who made you feel like shit. But what are we to learn when trapped in small spaces with no windows to see if the sun has strength enough to climb over thick clouds and eagle's feathers? What do we gather when shit happens? How does the caterpillar survive when anger fills its small living quarters? When heat intensifies, the caterpillar transforms to fly.

Ultimate Betrayal

Rejection is the holding back of rain when the earth is dying to live again. Pain does not know the feel of what could rise as a result of touching. Rejection has a unique way of leaving scars for years resulting in fear. Walls suffocate the heart trying to climb and sing again. Not only does life cease, but he who rests his head upon her breast also ceases to hear, rejecting any further touching. It's painful to think of those who only love us for what we can give only to leave our hands empty. When our doors close and lock and we are faced with silence, realizing that everyone is happy except us, that eventually intensifies how lonely we feel. As painful as this may be, it is better to be rejected by others than to reject our truest self which is our ultimate betrayal.

In Love Once

I was in love once (I, who was anti-relationship, fell in love). My heart sang so loud until my lover heard it. Morning, noon, and night were shared with the love we had between us. I believe the sun got jealous because it no longer shone upon my face alone but ours upon our pillows. But when my heart was broken by the one I loved, I cried. I almost drowned in my salty rain before the smog lifted. The smell, the touch, and the whisper from my ex-lover were soon replaced by cold sheets and painful memories. When I bellowed like a wounded animal, I didn't realize that my tears were penetrating that dirty place of mine, fertilizing those sleeping seeds of love waiting within me to be awaken. Now I am a part of that which grows stronger, blooming in the arms of another.

ABOUT THE AUTHOR

Donovan Stokes was raised in historically rich Charleston, South Carolina, where as a young boy he would walk along King Street and watch life in the South colored with a sensitive and spiritual nature. He felt the pangs of an oppressed soul and longed for a better life. One day while traveling, he noticed weeds growing through cracks in a sidewalk and marveled how weak but strong they were growing from such difficulty. That simple thought gave him inspiration in seeking new directions through life in the military and college where he would eventually earn a Bachelor's degree in Social Science and Education.

While attending college, Donovan kept a journal of his deepest feelings and desires. His strongest motivation was to be of service to his fellow man in helping those less fortunate. He found great insight to his own life through the feel of poetry. His inspiration for writing was formulated from great poets such as Maya Angelou, author of *I Know Why the Cage Bird Sings*, Robert Frost, author of *The Road Less Traveled*, and Mark Nepo, author of *The Book of Awakening*.

The poetry Donovan Stokes has penned across the pages of this book and the years of his life speak of a young man rising from despair and disappointment with a soul planted deep in faith and trust in something far greater than himself. He is lifted to a level beyond where he began to a place of strength and hope.

Made in the USA
Lexington, KY
11 May 2018